W9-BPC-638

HAYES TECHNOLOGY SERIES

SPACE TOUR

WRITTEN BY: DAN MACKIE

ILLUSTRATED BY: MARK HUGHES

RICK ROWDEN

CHARLES E. BASTIEN

DESIGNED BY: MARK HUGHES

©1986 Hayes Publishing Ltd., Burlington, Ontario

ISBN 0-88625-103-6

Hayes Publishing Ltd., 3312 Mainway, Burlington, Ontario L7M 1A7

CONTENTS

Canadian Cataloguing in Publication Data

Mackie, Dan.
   Space tour
              ISBN 0-88625-103-6.

1. Outer space - Exploration - Juvenile
literature. I. Title.

TL793.M32 1985   j629.4'1   C85-098434-3

ABOUT THIS BOOK

We have called this book "Space Tour" because as it is being written, we are at the dawn of travel in space for pleasure and profit. Already, plans have been made for 60-seat space shuttle flights from the United States which will be capable of transporting tourists into orbit to view the construction and operation of space stations, to see the moon from the clarity of near space, to gaze upon the earth, to see entire continents pass slowly below.

Or is it above? There is no sense of up or down in space because there is no gravity. Just imagine how that must feel! When you look at the earth there is only a sense of moving towards, away or past, but never down! How do we adjust our senses to that?

SPACE TOUR is a book of facts and predictions about space travel. There is a very real possibility that you will travel in space yourself. When you read this book, then, imagine that you are preparing for your first flight in space.

Imagine? No, that is the wrong word. In reading SPACE TOUR you will be preparing yourself for spaceflight! It is going to happen, just as surely as flight itself happened. So read on -- and prepare yourself!

COUNTDOWN TO LIFTOFF

As you can imagine, sending a rocket with its payload into orbit is pretty tricky business. All you have to do is watch Mission Control as it is being shown on TV to feel the tension that is generated by all the activity that precedes a launch. We have become accustomed over the years to learn space launch phrases like "All systems go" and "We have ignition" and "We have liftoff!"

In between all that and the commentators on the television, you keep hearing times announced like "T minus 9 -- All systems go," and so forth. Finally, you hear the familiar countdown to liftoff. Have you ever wondered what all the various times mean? Let's run through a typical space shuttle countdown so that you will know what's up when you take your first space trip.

T-11 hr.
The countdown sequence begins eleven hours before liftoff, when a large structure known as the Rotating Service Structure is swung away from the space shuttle and its rockets. It has been used to service the shuttle and its payload. You should be in bed asleep when this happens, although you might be too excited to sleep much!

T-5 hr. 30 min.
Launch pad is cleared of all loose objects and people.

T-5 hr.
Actual countdown begins (with announcements). The liquid oxygen and hydrogen transfer system is cooled down. Everything has to be very cold before the fuel is loaded because the hydrogen and oxygen are kept at -251°C and -147.2°C, and to just pump these into a warm pipeline system and tanks would cause them to vaporize.

T-4 hr. 30 min.
Oxygen filling is begun.

T-2 hr. 50 min.
Hydrogen filling is begun. Meanwhile, you finish your breakfast with the crew.

T-2 hr. 4 min.
You begin the entry procedures. You have difficulty in controlling the butterflies in your stomach as you begin dressing in your space outfit. Then you begin a ride to the launch pad and up its elevator.

T-1 hr. 5 min.
You are inside the space shuttle, along with the pilot, commander, mission specialist, payload specialist and main cabin attendant. You hear them close and lock the door. Waiting through the countdown seems like eternity to you! Meanwhile, the crew is busy checking for cabin leaks. This takes a long time. (Until T-25 min.)

T-30 min.
Whew! Things are moving faster than you realized. You do not know it, but the final closing up of the facilities at the launch pad is in progress. All ground crew have to get into the holdback area by T-10 min.

T-25 min.
Communications checks are made between Mission Control and the crew. A final weather briefing is given.

T-20 min.
The computers are loaded with the flight program.

T-9 min.
Automatic launch sequence is started.

T-7 min.
Crew access platform is withdrawn from the space shuttle.

T-5 min.
Activate shuttle hydraulic units. You can hear some noises inside the shuttle! (Gulp!)

T-4 min. 30 sec.
Orbiter goes to internal power. More noises, lights flicker.

T-3 min.
Gimbal main engines to start position. Away below you the nozzles on the rockets position themselves, pointing in the right direction for startup.

T-2 min. 55 sec.
Oxygen tank is being adjusted to flight pressure.

T-2 min. 30 sec.
Oxygen vent line is disconnected.

T-1 min. 57 sec.
Hydrogen tank is adjusted to flight pressure.

T-25 sec.
Solid rocket booster hydraulic units are turned on, although you can't hear them because they are too far below.

T-18 sec.
Solid rocket booster nozzle profile is checked.

T-3.46 to 3.22 sec.
Ignition! Solid rocket boosters are started. The shuttle begins to shake. It sounds like a huge thunderstorm outside.

T-0
Main engines are roaring now, and the whole place is shaking like it is going to come apart. The engines are at 90% power! You are either excited or terrified; you don't know which!

T+2.64
Just when you are beginning to think that this machine will never move, there is an explosion outside as the holddown bolts are triggered, releasing the shuttle and its engines from their moorings.

T+3 sec.
We have liftoff!

The noise outside is only matched by your heart pounding in your ears! This is the most exciting moment of your life. And, what's more, it is going to get even more exciting! Holy mackerel!!!

SPACE — WHAT IS IT?

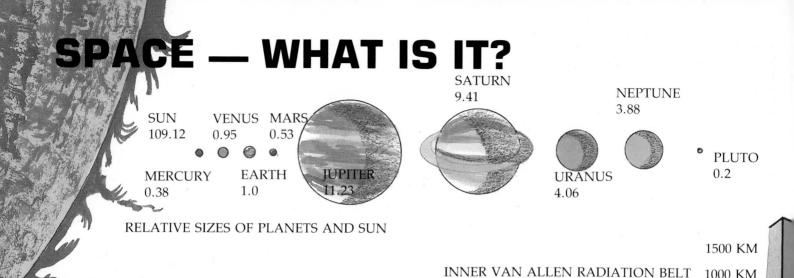

RELATIVE SIZES OF PLANETS AND SUN

Have you ever lain on your back on a clear summer night and stared up into space and wondered just where does it end? Does it go on forever?

To put things into the perspective of your space tour, we have to realize that we can only travel in space to the limits of the human life span. We are part of a solar system that consists of the sun, surrounded by nine planets and their moons that are in orbit around the sun. Our solar system, including our sun, is one of trillions which form a galaxy known as the Milky Way . Our galaxy is only one of trillions of galaxies in the universe!   So, when we talk about a space tour in this book, we are talking about traveling to places that will likely be reached during your life -- to our planets and their moons.

Now, let's begin our space tour. If we just fly out into space, will we be safe? How come we have to wear a spacesuit?

To begin with, the earth is surrounded by a layer of air that we breathe, which consists of about 78% nitrogen and 21% oxygen. This layer is only about 10 km (about 32,000 feet) thick. It gradually peters out, getting thinner and thinner with altitude. After 10 km, the air is so thin that it cannot be breathed. It dissipates to 50 km (164,000 feet) above the earth to a layer of ozone. This band of air and earth gases is known as the stratosphere. If we don't wear a breathing apparatus out here, we will suffocate and die.

We also need a spacesuit to protect us from dangerous ultraviolet radiation as we move beyond the ozone layer into space. The next 450 km surrounding the earth consists of ionized air and charged particles from the sun in various layers. This area is known as the ionosphere. A further 1,000 km at the edge of a band called the Exosphere, a band of radiation known as the Inner Van Allen Radiation Belt exists. This also traps radiation from the sun.

1500 KM

INNER VAN ALLEN RADIATION BELT   1000 KM

EXOSPHERE

AREA OF SPACE SHUTTLE'S OPERATIONAL ORBITS

LOW MANNED SPACECRAFT ORBITS   500 KM

IONOSPHERE

AURORA BOREALIS (NORTHERN HEMISPHERE)

OZONE LAYER   100 KM

FILTERS ULTRAVIOLET RADIATION

50 KM

METEORS BURN UP HERE

STRATOSPHERE

25 KM

10 KM

CIRRUS CLOUDS

8848 M MOUNT EVEREST

CUMULUS CLOUDS

EARTH SURFACE

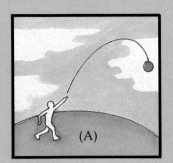 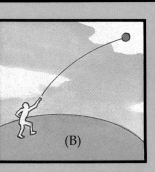 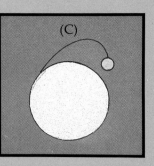

Okay, now that we've got all this heavy gear on, how are we going to leap into space? How do we get our spacecraft, which weighs many tons, into orbit?

Gravity holds us on the earth and gives us weight.

The farther you go from the earth, the less you would weigh until finally you would become weightless. When you become weightless, you have escaped the gravity of the earth. And you are in space!

As long as you are in orbit about the earth, you are under the influence of the earth's gravity.(A) Imagine throwing a ball up in the air along the length of a football field.It begins to arc towards the ground, because the force of the earth's gravity is pulling it down. (B) Even if you could throw it hard enough, it would leave the earth and go into outer space, but it would initially curve before it left the

earth because in the beginning of its flight the earth is trying to pull it down.

(C) If you could throw the ball hard enough to just travel fourteen thousand miles along the earth, it would orbit half of the earth.(D) If you threw it a little harder so that it went twice as far, then it would go right around the globe. It would be in orbit.

For an object (or satellite) to be in orbit, its speed, relative to earth, must be such that the centrifugal force caused by its circular path must exactly balance the pull of the earth. If the satellite is traveling too slow, it will be out of balance and fall to earth. If it is traveling too fast, it will drift away from the earth until it is in balance. If it is traveling fast enough, it will drift far enough from the earth to escape its gravity altogether. At that point it will be in outer space.

But, just as the earth's gravity pulled at the satellite or object, so would the gravity of other planets and moons and asteroids. This must be taken into account when traveling into space. If you traveled too near a moon, for example, and you were not traveling fast enough, it would pull you to it. In any case, its gravitational pull would alter your flight path.

ASTRONAUTS

WHAT IS AN ASTRONAUT?

Your space shuttle commander will be an astronaut.

When Americans first began training men to travel into space, they were dubbed "astronauts" by scientists.

The Russians, however, who were first in space, dubbed their spacemen and women "cosmonauts." America decided to stick to the term astronaut.

HOW ARE ASTRONAUTS TRAINED?

Most astronauts graduate from universities in sciences or engineering, taking courses that are strong in mathematics, chemistry, physics, biology and sometimes in languages.

Although early space capsule astronauts were expected to do little in their spaceflights, a modern space shuttle astronaut, such as the one who is commanding your space tour, needs to be trained in advanced flying, usually logging several thousand hours of flying jets to prepare him for transition to space shuttles.

During their training at the National Aeronautics and Space Administration (NASA), American astronauts undergo intense physical testing such as:

- testing for claustrophobia (fear of enclosed spaces)
- testing for resistance to "g" forces
- testing for resistance to motion sickness
- testing for ability to cope with weightlessness

An astronaut on a space shuttle has to study and become expert on the contents of over 200 books in order to prepare for his flight. In addition, he has to work out every day, eat the right foods and be sure to sleep regular hours.

WHAT DOES AN ASTRONAUT DO?

Astronauts are working spaceship pilots who do other things besides helping to take the ship or space shuttle into space and back again. They will show you the cockpit, its controls and instruments and show you how it all works, once you are safely in orbit. Since most space shuttle trips are for several days, the astronaut must also maintain the operation of the shuttle during its stay in space, keeping it clean, tending the air supply system, the power supply, food supply, sewage disposal, health care, etc. The crew can show you how that all works, but there are over 2,300 knobs and buttons that you are not allowed to touch!

FAMOUS ASTRONAUTS AND COSMONAUTS

The first astronaut in space was Russian cosmonaut, Yuri Gagarin, who orbited the earth on April 12, 1961, in a capsule called Vostok I.

Alan Shepard was the first American in space. He made a suborbital flight on May 5, 1961, in a capsule called Freedom 7.

Less than one year later, John Glenn went into orbit in Friendship 7 on February 20, 1962.

On June 16, 1963, Valentina Tereshkova orbited the earth in the Russian spaceship, Vostok 6, becoming the first woman in space.

Cosmonaut Alexei Leonov of the Soviet Union made the first space walk on March 18, 1965. He spent 20 minutes tethered outside Voshkod 2.

Neil Armstrong and David Scott of the United States made the first space docking while aboard Gemini 8 on March 16, 1966. They linked up with an Agena target vehicle.

On January 27, 1967, Virgil Grissom, Edward White and Roger Chaffee became the first casualties of the space program. They died in a fire while still on the launch pad at the Kennedy Space Center.

Vladimir Kovarov of the U.S.S.R. died on a mission when Soyuz I got entangled in its parachute while attempting to land on April 24, 1967.

American astronauts Neil Armstrong and Edwin Aldrin became the first men to land on the moon on July 20, 1969. Their ship was the Apollo II.

On July 17, 1975, Americans Tom Stafford, Vance Brand and Deke Slayton linked their Apollo spaceship up with a Russian Soyuz while in orbit, where they shook hands with Russians Alexei Leonov and Valerie Kubasov.

On April 12, 1981, the first flight of the American Space Shuttle Enterprise took place, carrying John Young and Robert Crippen, taking off from Cape Canaveral.

Are you going to be the first kid in space?

ENGINES

Your space shuttle with boosters weighs close to 2,000 tons at takeoff. That is heavier than three locomotives, a small ship or a ferryboat! Yet, its engines must be capable of "throwing" it into orbit. Just think of that as you try to throw a ball as high as you can.

HOW DOES A ROCKET WORK?

When you travel to space, your rockets operate like the jet engines on a plane -- the pressure of burning gases inside the engines builds up, pushing outwards in all directions. The gases are allowed to escape through a nozzle at the rear of the engine. Since it is

ONE OF THREE MAIN SHUTTLE ENGINES (S.S.M.E.)

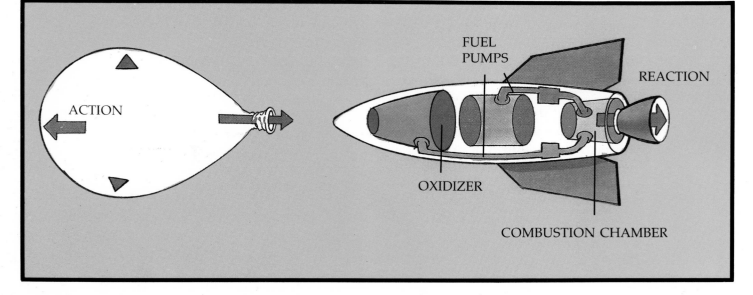

pushing against the engine on one side and air or space at the other, it creates a net force that moves the engine exactly as air escaping from a balloon propels it forward.

Liquid fuel rocket engines burn a liquid fuel in the presence of oxygen. Since there is no oxygen in space, the rocket engine carries its own oxygen which is cooled and squeezed down to liquid form. Rockets usually use liquid hydrogen, also cooled and compressed to liquid form.

What does hydrogen become when it is burned (oxidized) in the presence of oxygen? What is all that "smoke" coming out of the nozzle at the end of the rocket? If you guessed or figured out that it was water -- as water

vapor or steam -- then you were correct! Water, you see, is composed of hydrogen and oxygen.

Solid rockets, on the other hand, use chlorine as an oxidizer. It is mixed with the fuel and a catalyst and a binder while in liquid form and then dried so that in the end it becomes a solid that looks and feels like a hard rubber eraser. The propellant is known as PBAN, but if you want to dazzle your friends, try to memorize its full name:

"polybutadiene acrylic acid acrytonitrile terpolymer."

The actual fuel being burned is simply aluminum powder.

10

SPACE ENGINES

An engine is a device that moves an object from one place to another, using energy in some form. Usually, that energy is in the form of heat, like burning gasoline. Gravity, too, is a form of energy known as potential energy. It can cause an object to move or fall or roll down a hill or glide on a cushion of air. When your spaceship returns to earth, it uses the earth's gravity as an engine to pull it down.

Gravity can also be used in outer space to save rocket fuel. If you wanted to go to a far-out planet, for example, you could plan your flight so that its path comes close to a nearer planet. You would already have enough speed to prevent its gravity from capturing you, yet its gravity would pull you towards it, increasing your speed. It's like using the nearby planet as a slingshot to boost your speed instead of using up rocket fuel.

Nuclear engines are barred by an international treaty that forbids the detonation of nuclear devices in space, but it is expected that nuclear engines will be used in the future.

Ion engines also need a nuclear power source to provide electricity and heat. Nuclear energy is used to ionize mercury atoms. These ions are accelerated out the rear of the engine by electricity and, because of the heavy weight of the ions, the engine is thrust forward.

Energy from the sun has been used by man for some time on earth.

It may be possible to use the sun's energy to power a mercury ion engine .

It has been proposed that very thin, light sails made of foil could be used to get free engine power from the sun. They would be huge, of course, but what does that matter? In space, there is no gravity, so it would be easy to unfurl them and hold them up.

11

SATELLITES

IS AN ORBIT A CIRCLE?

When you go into space in your shuttle for the first time, you may be surprised to learn that your astronauts do a little more than ride the ship into orbit. Once you get into orbit, your commander will probably begin maneuvering the shuttle in two ways. First, he will adjust the ship so that it is orientated in line with the orbit and "rightside up" with respect to the earth. Then, he will adjust the orbit so that it is circular instead of an ellipse!

Why?

An ellipse is really just two arcs joined together. Remember your experiment of throwing a ball in the air? Does it not "arc" back down? If you threw it into orbit, it would come down on the other side of the earth, and rise up in another arc. This continuous up-down action makes the shape of an ellipse (a football shape). A circular orbit, however, is much more practical for satellites.

HOW FAST IS AN ORBIT?

As we said earlier, it is the curved flight around a planet that equalizes the gravitational pull of the planet. It is a kind of balancing act. The closer we are to the planet or earth, the faster we have to go to balance the gravitational force.

The simplest orbit is the elliptical orbit. You can circumvent one or more planets or moons in a single orbit, but it changes the shape of the orbit.

If, for example, you orbited the earth and moon together, the apogee (the highest point of the arc) above the earth would be different than the apogee above the moon because the gravitational pull of the moon is only one-sixth the pull of the earth. (Gravitational pull is in proportion to the weight or mass of a body.) In effect, you have two ellipses that are blended.

Circular orbits can be at any angle and direction with respect to the earth. The earth, itself, rotates on its axis from west to east so that a satellite traveling in an orbit that is heading east would appear to an observer on the ground to be traveling much slower than it would if it were traveling in an orbit that is heading west. In fact, a satellite that is positioned to be directly 35,880 km (22,300 miles) above the equator and heading east,

ELLIPTICAL ORBIT

EQUATORIAL ORBIT

GEOSTATIONARY ORBIT

SUN-SYNCHRONOUS ORBIT

POLAR ORBIT

U.S.S.R. ORBIT

LOW EARTH ORBIT (LEO)

SHUTTLE RELEASES SATELLITE FROM LEO TO GEO
SATELLITE STAYS AT SAME POINT ABOVE EARTH
GEOSYNCHRONOUS ORBIT (GEO)

HEIGHT ABOVE EARTH	SPEED OF ORBIT
161 KM (100 MI.)	28,163 KPH (17,500 MPH)
805 KM (500 MI.)	26,553 KPH (16,500 MPH)
16,093 KM (10,000 MI.)	15,288 KPH (9,500 MPH)
THE MOON:	
382,000 KM (237,000 MI.)	3,620 KPH (2,250 MPH)

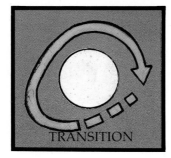

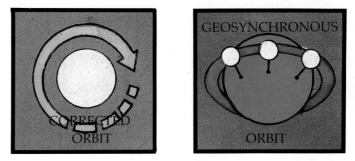

would appear to be stationary to an observer on earth. This is because the earth's rotation happens to be the same speed as that needed to keep such a satellite in orbit.

Such orbits are called Geosynchronous orbits. They were originated by British scientist and great science-fiction writer, Arthur C. Clarke. Communication satellites are usually in Geosynchronous orbits.

TYPES OF SATELLITES

The first satellite, Sputnik I, was merely used to demonstrate that an object could be put into orbit. It had a transmitter on it that sent a beeping signal.

A lot of early satellites were used to find out what near space was like, what were the problems in space and how to adapt to them.

If your space tour were to take you to each and every satellite, you would be old and gray by the time you visited all of them. There are more than 2,500 in orbit and over 4,500 remnants -- so-called space "junk." The most common satellite you would find would be the communications satellite -- the one that transmitted the Winter Olympics from Sarajevo to Los Angeles, for example.

Some satellites are used for mapping, transmitting pictures to earth electronically. A picture of a coin on the ground can be taken from 100 miles up that is so clear that you can tell whether it is heads or tails! Naturally, such satellites are used for spying.

Many satellites are used to measure forests, or to find mineral deposits. Others can be used for navigating ships and aircraft.

Almost all satellites use solar panels to extract energy from the sun. The electricity produced powers the cameras. Satellites like those have funny bat wings or weird antennae, making them look like bugs. If you drift by one, you may feel like swatting it!

The Anik series of satellites are somewhat different. They are shaped like a soup can with the lid open. The sides of the can spin and have solar panels where the soup label would be. It spins so that it remains stable, exactly as a gyroscope on a string. The lid is really an antenna for receiving and relaying signals from the earth.

HOW ARE SATELLITES PUT INTO ORBIT?

Many satellites are fired into orbit by multistage rockets, such as the Ariane which is used by the European Space Agency. They put satellites into orbit from French Guiana, many of them the communication satellites.

Larger and more complex satellites like the Anik are usually put into orbit by the space shuttle.

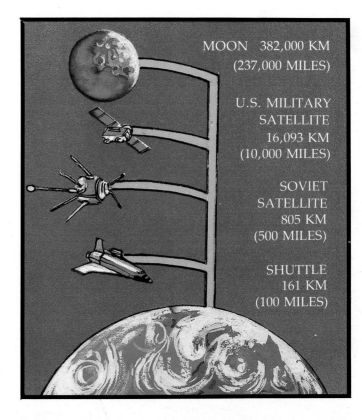

MOON 382,000 KM (237,000 MILES)

U.S. MILITARY SATELLITE 16,093 KM (10,000 MILES)

SOVIET SATELLITE 805 KM (500 MILES)

SHUTTLE 161 KM (100 MILES)

THE SHUTTLE CONCEPT

HOW THE SPACE SHUTTLE WORKS

1 To get into orbit, the space shuttle uses its own engines as well as two solid-fuel booster rockets.

7 Finally, the shuttle slows down, cools off somewhat and begins to glide at quite a steep (22-degree) angle. The control surfaces begin to react just like that of an airplane, and the pilot guides it towards the landing strip, turning this way and that so that he will be at the right height. Slowing the shuttle down to about 320 kph (200 mph), the pilot steers the craft onto the runway where its air brakes and wheel brakes bring it to a halt. Down -- safe and sound!

2 The solid-fuel rockets are used to get the shuttle started and to a height of about 50 km (31 miles). At that point, the boosters have nearly burnt all of their fuel, so they are jettisoned by firing two small rockets to move them away from the main shuttle. A small parachute pops out, pulling three large parachutes out after it, lowering the boosters gently to the sea. Tugboats latch onto the rockets and tow them back to land where they will be refurbished for the next mission.

6 As it descends to 120,000 meters (400,000 feet), it heats up as it enters the atmosphere. This is caused by the friction of air. Don't forget that it is traveling at 25 times the speed of sound! The shuttle has special tiles glued to its underside to resist the heat and protect the people inside. They begin to glow red hot as they reach 1500°C, but the people inside remain cool. At that point, the heat prevents any communication with Mission Control, and there is a period of radio silence.

3 Just before the boosters are jettisoned the main engines power up and begin to take over the job of accelerating. The engines are fed by a huge fuel tank that is eventually discarded and burns up in the atmosphere. It is the only part of the space shuttle that cannot be re-used.

Once the tank has been discarded, the shuttle coasts for awhile, then its engines are fired again, using fuel from internal tanks, to trim it out at orbital velocity, which is 7,847 meters per second (17,500 mph). This puts the shuttle into an elliptical orbit. Once it has traveled halfway around the earth, the rockets fire again, adjusting the shape of the orbit from elliptical to circular.

4 At that point, the shuttle is orbiting at about 180 km (112 miles) above the earth, ready to do the job that it was sent into space to do. In fact, the orbit height could be 160 km (100 miles) to 960 km (600 miles), depending on the payload and the job. Usually, the shuttle is used to put other objects into orbit, retrieve satellites for repair or repositioning, to transport people and materials to a space station or, as in your case, to simply take people on a space tour.

5 When the shuttle is ready to go to work, two huge doors open that are almost the full length of the shuttle. A mechanical arm, called the Canadarm because it was built in Canada, lifts satellites out of the cargo bay, setting them up for positioning into orbit. A communications satellite, for example, may be launched by its own rocket engine from the cargo bay. The Canadarm points it in the right direction, the satellite begins spinning, and it is started off by springs. Once it is a safe distance away from the shuttle, its rockets are fired, sending it into orbit far above the shuttle.

Its work done, the Canadarm retracts into the cargo bay, the doors close, and the crew begin to prepare the ship for return to earth. The first thing they will do is a weather check with NASA ground stations to find out if they should land at the Kennedy Space Center in Florida or Vandenberg Air Force Base in California. Once cleared for descent, the pilot will maneuver the shuttle so that it is orbiting backwards, then fire its rockets so that it will begin slowing down, losing its orbital velocity which will start it back towards earth. As it begins to lose height, the pilot reverses the shuttle again so that it is pointing in the right direction, but nose high. It is beginning to transform from an orbiter to a glider!

SPACE STATIONS

Both Skylab and Salyut had the problem of not being retrievable. In other words, once they are in orbit, they cannot be brought back to earth for repairs or changes. Spacelab solves all that.

The first Spacelab was built by ten European countries who joined together as the European Space Agency (ESA). Carried aloft by the NASA space shuttle in 1983, it consisted of a room and a pallet attached to the shuttle which opened its cargo bay doors so that the European scientists could conduct experiments in space while working in a shirtsleeve atmosphere. Instruments and experiments that are meant to be exposed to space conditions are located on the pallet.

Spacelab modules are brought to earth, repaired, changed to different configurations, exchanged and sent back up, all over a

SKYLAB

In 1973, NASA put a space station into orbit. It was called Skylab. It was made of leftover hardware from the Apollo moon landing program. The outer shell had been made from a Saturn V rocket casing.

American scientists and astronauts made three trips to Skylab after it had been placed into orbit, performing many experiments and setting endurance records of 28, 59 and 84 days in orbit. Eventually, Skylab was abandoned, and it came down over Australia where it broke up and burned in the atmosphere.

SALYUT

Meanwhile, the Russians developed an orbiting space station called Salyut, which they supplied with teams of cosmonauts by Soyuz spacecraft. By adding modules to Salyut, which is like adding rooms, they increased its size so that their cosmonauts could live more comfortably. They supplied the space station with a robot ferry called Progress and set an endurance record in 1982 when two cosmonauts spent 211 days in orbit.

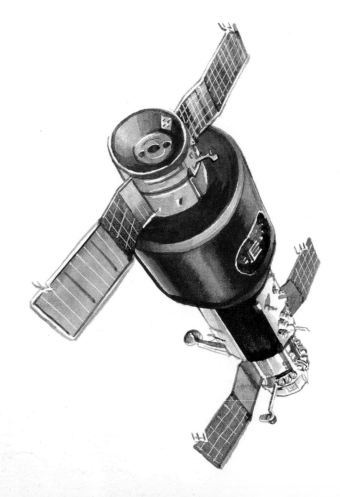

two-week period! Perhaps on your space tour you will pass one or see one of its astronauts outside, flying about in his manned maneuvering unit.

By making modules to fit the cargo bay of a space shuttle, an orbiting space station can be built by joining the modules together in a similar fashion to Salyut, except that modules can be taken off and returned to earth for changes and repairs. Each module can be a room for a special purpose such as a laboratory, bedrooms, galley or kitchen, recreation room, etc.

Imagine playing table tennis in weightlessness! You would have to have your feet strapped to the floor. Your shots would definitely have to be "down" at the table, although with weightlessness, the effects of spinning the ball would be phenomenal!

SPACE PLATFORMS

Construction of space platforms 400 km (250 miles) above the earth and higher is done with beams that can be extremely light because of weightlessness in space. In fact, the beams can be made in space from rolls of aluminum that are folded and formed in space on a special machine.

Your space commander may take you out on a manned maneuvering unit to tour such a construction site. There you will see workmen zinging around the construction; however, they won't be wearing the usual hard hats that you see on earth!

Space stations and space platforms will increase in size as more and more uses for them have been determined. While most space stations nowadays are experimental, future stations will be set up for manufacturing, for use as satellite repair stations and for power plants. The first major service center will be put into operation in 1992. It will be built by a consortium made up of NASA, ESA, Japan and Canada. It will be about 500 feet long, have huge sail-like panels for capturing solar energy, living quarters, laboratory, manufacturing space, storage, a control center and a dock for space shuttles. Orbit height will be 300 km (185 miles) above earth.

Larger structures are planned that would orbit 36,000 km (22,300 miles) above earth. One such project will be a mammoth solar power station requiring about 100,000 tons of material to build.

FUTURE EXPLORATION

According to calculations, the nearest star is 250 light years away. To travel there and back at the speed of light would take 500 years! All of this is based on the assumption that we can travel at the speed of light, and we're not so sure that we can!

Exploring the stars, then, may be possible, but we would have to build a starship that is a world in itself, replenishing its own energy and food and water. People would be born, live and die on such an exploration.

In the very near future, manned exploration will probably remain within our own solar system. Starships, if they are ever built, will probably just be space probes.

MANNED SPACE EXPLORATION

Only the moon has been explored by man. Neil Armstrong and Edwin Aldrin were the first on the moon using the Apollo II. Five other flights carrying two men each explored the moon, the last being in 1972, making a total of twelve men to walk on the moon.

Space platforms are a logical stage in development of manned space exploration. Perhaps a moonbase will be a further stepping stone to other planets such as Mars.

That brings up the question: If we are to travel into space, where should we go?

Mercury, Venus and Mars are known as terrestial planets, which means that they are made up of earth-like materials.

Mercury is the closest to the Sun and rotates slowly, making it either too hot (425°C) or too cold (-175°C) to explore, and it has little atmosphere.

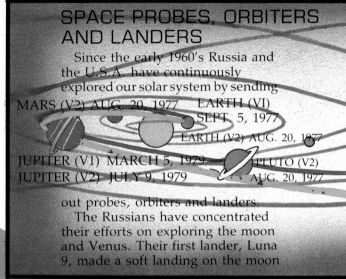

SPACE PROBES, ORBITERS AND LANDERS

Since the early 1960's Russia and the U.S.A. have continuously explored our solar system by sending

MARS (V2) AUG. 20, 1977   EARTH (VI)
                            SEPT. 5, 1977
                            EARTH (V2) AUG. 20, 1977
JUPITER (V1) MARCH 5, 1979   PLUTO (V2)
JUPITER (V2) JULY 9, 1979   AUG. 20, 1977

out probes, orbiters and landers. The Russians have concentrated their efforts on exploring the moon and Venus. Their first lander, Luna 9, made a soft landing on the moon

Venus is even hotter and is surrounded by a poisonous, carbon dioxide atmosphere saturated with sulfuric acid droplets. Not a good place to spend the weekend!

Mars is a likely place to explore, even though it, too, has little oxygen in its atmosphere. And at night it goes down to -75°C, so bundle up! It would take about seven months to get there, too, so you had better pack a king-sized lunch!

Other possibilities for manned exploration are Jupiter and one of Saturn's moons, Titan. It has an atmosphere; however, you couldn't breathe it!

All of this sounds impossibly difficult, but we are encouraged by knowing that the more we explore, the more we know. Perhaps we should begin slowly. First with a space platform, then the moonbase. Then a Mars base? Who knows, that might lead to discovery of another planet or a habitable moon!

NEPTUNE (V2)
SEPT. 1, 1989

URANUS (V2)
JAN. 27, 1986

Early U.S. efforts were directed towards Mars. The Mariner 4 flew by Mars in 1965. In the early 1970's Pioneer 10 and 11 were launched to study Jupiter. America's first soft landing on another planet was made on Mars by Viking 2, sending back spectacular pictures of Marscape in 1976, followed by landing on Venus

VOYAGER 2

in 1966. The Russians tried twice to land on Mars, but both landers failed just before impact. Since then their orbiters, probes and landers, the Venera series, have continuously studied Venus, putting a lander on Venus as early as 1970.

VOYAGER 1

in 1978. Meanwhile, Voyager 1 and 2 probes have studied Jupiter and Saturn and should be sending back information about Uranus in 1986 and Neptune in 1989.

SOLAR PANEL
POWER STATION

FUTURE USE OF SPACE

If we continue to grow in population at our present growth rate, we would run out of a place to stand after the year 2056! Friday, November 13th, to be exact. Moving to the moon wouldn't do much good because at the same growth rate, it would only give us another 35 years. There are other planets, but living on them may not be all that great.

No, looking to outer space to find new land is not the answer to our population problems. We have to look for other solutions right here on earth.

MANUFACTURING

As you tour Spacelab in your travels, you will learn that a whole host of things have been discovered to be made better in space than on earth, in many cases because of the absence of gravity. Here is a list of things that can be made in space better than on earth:

-- mixtures of heavy and light metals or other materials
-- crystals of all kinds
-- some vaccines
-- metal "sponge" (metal and air mixed, then solidified)
-- improved glasses and ceramics
-- semi-conductors
-- super lenses

EARTH WATCH

Using special cameras, you can take a picture of a car and read its license plate from space! More important vigils on the earth are made from space, however, such as finding mineral resources, locating oil fields, studying vegetation, finding fish, locating lost ships or airplanes, predicting weather, locating forest fires and predicting crop production.

Satellites also provide the essential link of the peoples of the world through telephone, radio and television.

SPACE WATCH

A telescope mounted on a satellite is free of the distortions caused by dust, pollution, clouds and heat waves in our atmosphere, giving much more clarity.

SPACE POWER

Solar power can be collected in huge panels, focused on a steam turbine which creates electricity. This electricity can be turned into microwaves, beamed to earth where it can be collected in huge dishes, and converted back to electricity. This would be a pollution-free method of making electricity, although at this point we are not sure of the effect of microwaves on the atmosphere.

SPACE TOURISM

They may be just building the first hotel in space as you make your tour. You might think they won't have a swimming pool in it because of weightlessness, but don't be too sure! The pool will be inside a revolving cylinder so that the water will remain, say, six feet deep along the walls due to the centrifugal force. To "dive"

LIVING LEVEL

ROTATING SPACE COLONY

SERVICE LEVELS

in you have to float along the center of the cylinder, then step out on a revolving ladder. Once you begin to feel the centrifugal force, you can let go and you will "fall" in. Don't do a belly flop!

SPACE MEDICINE

Weightlessness is a perfect place to be if you have major burns on your body because you can float without touching anything, giving your burns a chance to heal.

CITIES IN SPACE

Eventually, whole cities will evolve in space to service power stations, grow special foods and do special manufacturing, medicine and so on. These will house about 10,000 people. They will have farms and running water. These cities will probably be built as huge, torus-shaped (doughnut-shaped) so that they can revolve, creating artificial gravity.

EXTRATERRESTRIAL INTELLIGENCE

According to the astronomer Carl Sagan, there is about a 50-50 chance that there is intelligent life within our galaxy, and that it is likely to be about 250 light years away. So you can bet that you won't see any little green men on our space tour!

The idea that there is not anyone else in the universe seems so unacceptable to us that we usually are easily convinced that extraterrestrial life is a certainty. Sightings of UFO's have been happening since the notion of outer space began. Tens of thousands of sightings have been reported, yet only a handful cannot be explained. Even with the evidence against UFO's being overwhelming, we continue to grasp at the possibility.

Besides UFO sightings, there are many, many occurrences in history that have explanations that are logical but are theoretical only. Two that come to mind are Stonehenge in England, which is believed to be a huge calendar, and the strange markings and "landing sites" in the Peruvian Andes. Some people claim that these were built for or by extraterrestrial beings. Who knows?

Scientists have always been puzzled by a genetic code that is common to all life on earth. It consists of twenty-six kinds of organic molecules sometimes known as the "alphabet of life." They reason that life must have begun at many different places on the earth at the same time and, if so, how come all life is the same? How come it didn't evolve differently? One theory is that life began on earth from bacterial spores from another planet. If that is so, did the spores arrive by themselves or were they brought here?

All of these questions and many more have spawned the science fiction industry. We have books and TV stories and movies about weird creatures encountered as visitors on earth or during spaceflight. It heightens our desire to find extraterrestrial beings, even though real evidence in favor of finding some is overwhelmingly against there being anything at all.

PROJECT CYCLOPS BEING ASSEMBLED ON THE MOON

Nevertheless, scientists realize that what we do not know about space far exceeds what we do know. And so they are trying to establish contact with other life by listening at the huge Arecibo radio/radar observatory in Puerto Rico. Also, Project Cyclops, a mammoth bank of receptor dishes, has been proposed to be built on earth or on the moon solely for listening to outer space.

A message has been sent towards the star cluster M13 which is 25,000 light years away, transmitting a binary code based on mathematics and including the genetic code of earth. This was sent from the Arecibo observatory on November 16, 1974. Will earth ever receive an answer?

ARECIBO OBSERVATORY, PUERTO RICO

STAR WARS

There has been a constant upgrading of warfare technology, mostly by the United States and the Soviet Union.

Since the end of World War II and the beginning of spaceflight in the 1950's, the East and West developed rockets designed to deliver warheads to each other. These were called ICBM's or Intercontinental Ballistic Missiles. Along with their development came more powerful nuclear warheads, and more sophisticated early warning systems to fend off the onslaught of incoming missiles. The whole idea was to prevent war, not to attack, because both sides would be wiped out! To that end, the buildup of arms has escalated to the point that there are about 100 tons of explosives in existence for every man, woman and child on earth!

COMMUNICATIONS

Initially, early warning against attack was done by radar. ICBM's were stored in underground silos throughout the United States. Central control was at Cheyenne Mountain in Colorado.

Spying was done from very high-flying aircraft, such as the U-2 and the SR-71 Blackbird, which took pictures and kept track of Soviet military movements. Naturally, the

ICBM

next step was to put communications satellites into orbit. Today, the United States military relies on satellites for 70% of its communications. Russia relies on satellites to a lesser extent because it has developed a larger network of ground-based installations.

The United States has three satellite systems for spying on the earth. These are the Big Bird, Close Look and KH-11. The Soviet Union has two systems.

19766

766

U.S. AIR FORCE

USAF

LOCKHEED SR-71 BLACKBIRD RECONNAISSANCE AIRCRAFT

SATELLITE WARS

The United States began developing an anti-satellite weapon (ASAT) in the Satellite Interceptor (SAINT) program.

Knocking out Russian communications satellites from earth is relatively easy compared to U.S. satellites. This is because U.S. military communications satellites are in geosynchronous orbits some 35,800 km (22,000 miles) above earth, while the Russian satellites are in circular or so-called Molniya orbits as close as 600 km (375 miles) to earth.

Satellite-based infrared sensors could detect missiles fired from earth by sensing the heat from their exhaust plumes. They could direct anti-missile missiles to their location or, better yet, fire a rocket directly at the missile using a conventional warhead that explodes into a shotgun blast, sending off multiple pellets of explosive devices as it got close to the missile.

Russia has an anti-satellite system known as SIS (Satellite Interceptor System). These are known as "killer satellites" and are guided by radar.

The United States has developed the Miniature Homing Vehicle (MHV), which is launched from an F-15 fighter plane. It does not have a large exhaust plume because it is launched from high altitude, and so can escape detection by infrared sensors.

In 1984 President Reagan of the United States announced the Strategic Defense Initiative (SDI) which became popularly known as "Star Wars." The SDI system relies on laser beams.

SOLAR-POWERED LASER SATELLITE

MISSILE ATTACKING

F-15 FIRES 2-STAGE MISSILE

SATELLITE WARHEAD DESTROYS MISSILE

FLIGHT PATH ADJUSTED BY TELESCOPE

LASER REFLECTIVE SATELLITE

1ST STAGE

2ND STAGE

ANTI-MISSILE SATELLITE

25

MOON BASE

GREENHOUSES

SHUTTLE AIRSTRIP

MODULAR SUB-LEVEL HOUSING

DRIVE-IN STORAGE

SLEEPING QUARTERS

LABORATORY

GARAGE

SHUTTLE LAUNCH AREA

Your space tour may not take you as far as the moon, but you can bet that you will be able to travel to the moon soon after the turn of the century. James Beggs, head of NASA, has predicted that in a speech.

Apollo and Luna missions to the moon have brought back quite a lot of information on our neighbor. Rock samples indicated that the moon rocks contain nickel, iron, aluminum and silicon. Most importantly, the rocks contain oxygen! That means there is a source of oxygen for breathing and for oxidizing

rocket fuel. It would be a question of mining the rock and processing it to extract the oxygen. It could be that water may be found, frozen underground. If that were the case, drinking water could be made from it and also hydrogen extracted for rocket fuel.

First moon bases will probably be in the relatively flat "seas" near the Leibnitz Mountains at the South Pole where the sun never sets. People would be housed 2 m (6 feet) beneath the soil in order to protect them from cosmic rays.

CARGO CAPSULE LAUNCH

OPEN-PIT MINE

SOLAR & NUCLEAR POWER STATION

TELESCOPE

HEAT AND AIR PROCESSING

Moon soil and conditions are excellent for growing vegetables. Greenhouses will be built of plastic bubbles. Tomatoes as large as watermelons are predicted as a result of the lower gravity on the moon. Liquid waste would provide water and nutrients for the soil. Carbon dioxide exhaust from housing complexes will be piped to the greenhouses for conversion by the plants into oxygen.

Energy will be taken from the sun by solar panels that rotate to face the sun at all times. This will be converted to electricity by steam turbines which will provide heat, light and energy to power mining and manufacturing machinery.

It is likely that exotic and perhaps ordinary metals and minerals will be mined on the moon. These can be shot into earth orbit in capsules.

Tourism will probably become an industry on the moon. It is entirely possible that lovers will take a stroll in the earthlight, to gaze at the stars!

It is a certainty that a moonbase will be used to study the universe. And the probability of using the moon as a launch pad for rockets to planets is without doubt.

27

PLANET BASE

A base on Mars seems inevitable as a stepping stone to other planets. It is the nearest planet to earth that has nearly habitable conditions, although it is cold (-75°C) at night and has practically no atmosphere. As it is 78,000,000 km (48,500,000 miles) from earth, it would take nearly seven months to get there.

Some scientists have suggested that Mars could be made habitable by a process known as terraforming. Since there is frozen water in the soil and polar icecaps, it has been speculated that an atmosphere could be created, even though it would still be thin due to the low gravity on Mars, which is about one-third to one-half that of Earth. By spreading the red dust of Mars on the polar icecaps and orbiting solar mirrors to focus sunlight on the icecaps, perhaps enough heat could be generated to create water. If temperatures could be created that are warm

MELTING POLAR CAP

SOLAR PANEL SATELLITES

GEODESIC AGRODOMES

TRANSPORT HAULING PAYDIRT FROM MINE

SMALL JET PACK UNIT

SMALL CLEARING DOZER

enough to melt ice, perhaps vegetation could be planted that would convert the carbon dioxide atmosphere of Mars into oxygen. Once a layer of atmosphere has begun, then the "greenhouse" effect may possibly warm the planet.

Whether or not such a grand scale is feasible is not known, nor does it sound likely, but the Marscape is enough like earth that portions of it at least could be converted to earth-like conditions.

Much of the moonbase technology learned from that first stepping stone would be applied to living on Mars. The oxygen, for example, could be mined, just as on the moon. Heat from solar collectors could melt the ice in the soil and the water could be stored in icebags for later use.

Unique problems would occur on Mars that would not appear on the moon. Since there is an atmosphere on Mars, it is sometimes subjected to violent sand storms. It is believed that the first Soviet mission to Mars fell victim to winds of 500 kph (310 mph). Underground housing may be the answer, and vegetable gardens would have to be protected.

The Soviets have suggested that a base could be set up on Phobos, one of the moons of Mars. That would give us a vantage point from which to learn more about Mars before setting up a space colony.

Just getting to Mars requires a complex spaceship that has a self-contained ecology, since a trip there and back would take about two years. The technology to make such a trip exists now; however, the cost would be too much for one country to bear.

Other possible space colonies could be set up on Titan which is the largest of Saturn's moons. It has an atmosphere that is made up mostly of nitrogen and methane gas, and it has ice in its rocky surface. Europa, a moon of Jupiter, has also been cited as a possible pioneer colony.

SUB-LEVEL HOUSING WITH RECTRACTABLE SHIELDS

SHUTTLE & AIRSTRIP

SURVEYOR PLANNING LANDSCAPING

29

IMPACT ON ORDINARY PEOPLE

We usually think of spaceflight merely as an exercise in pioneering, in exploring new places. To a large degree, that is true. Exploration is the impetus or main reason for going into space. But we are finding out very quickly that there is a lot more to it than that, and that the benefits to us here on earth are far more reaching than we at first imagined.

But that's only a small part of it. Since spaceflight uses very sophisticated materials and equipment, and more demands are placed on these with each thrust forward, an awesome amount of inventiveness has to go on. New materials and machines have to be invented. These, once invented, find uses on earth, which improve our way of life. Such things as better alloys, longer-lasting batteries, tiny reliable electronics components, better radios and television, better cameras -- the list of new inventions could fill this book!

Communications satellites are our biggest benefit at this point in time and will probably have the biggest impact on human lives. We, in the western world, use satellite communications to watch television and to telephone around the world. But people who have had no direct access to knowing what is going on in the world are suddenly being made aware. In one case, for example, broadcasts were made to 5,000 villages in India to people who had never seen a television set

before! And as more and more television programs are shared between the various countries of the world, perhaps it will lead us to a more harmonious planet.

In North America alone over 500,000 jobs have been created by the space program. Since space workers are usually well paid, they also tend to spend more money than the average worker. Their spending creates demands from the economy -- more automobiles, better houses, more homes and recreational appliances are bought -- and that creates even more jobs, which in turn make spenders, which in turn makes more jobs and so on. So before the first rocket is even fired, North America is a better place to live because of it.

As far as managing the planet earth, satellites have contributed greatly. Here is a partial list of the good satellites can do:

- Making it possible to receive television signals in every home on earth from every country and continent!
- Improving weather predictions.
- Predicting earthquakes.
- Monitoring silt buildup in rivers and lakes.
- Searching for mineral and oil resources.
- Measuring the use and misuse of forest reserves.
- Looking for oil slicks at sea.
- Search and rescue of ships and airplanes.
- Monitoring pollution.

VIEW OF DETROIT RIVER DELTA

INTELSAT IV
RELAYS TELEPHONE
CALLS & TELEVISION

VELA 6
DETECTS NUCLEAR
EXPLOSIONS ON
EARTH'S
SURFACE

LANDSAT 4 OBSERVES GEOLOGY,
AGRICULTURE & BATHYMETRY

SARSAT SEARCH AND RESCUE

I.E.V. OBSERVES DEEP SPACE
INVESTIGATING QUASARS & BLACK HOLES

ACKNOWLEDGMENTS

We wish to thank the following organizations and agencies for their assistance and for making available material from their collections:

NATIONAL AERONAUTICS AND SPACE ADMINISTRATION

SPAR AEROSPACE CORPORATION

GOVERNMENT OF U.S.S.R.

TELESAT CANADA

EUROPEAN SPACE AGENCY

NATIONAL RESEARCH COUNCIL OF CANADA

WEIGHTS AND MEASURES

There is a tendency towards using metric weights and measures worldwide, especially among scientists. However, North Americans in particular still think in terms of Imperial measures. Aircraft, for example, still have altimeters that show height above the earth in feet, and distances are measured in statute miles. In this book we will deal in both metric and Imperial measures. The following is a list of important comparisons:

1 meter (m) = 3.28 feet (ft.)
1 kilometer (km) = 0.62 miles (mi.)
1 kilogram (kg) = 2.2 pounds (lb.)
1 tonne = 1000 kilograms = 2200 lb.
1 knot (kt) = 1 nautical mile per hour
1 nautical mile (nm) = 1.15 statute miles (mi.)
1 liter (L) = 0.264 U.S. gallons (gal.)
Speed of light = 186,000 miles per second = 300,000,000 meters per second
(One light year is defined as the distance over which light can travel in one year's time = approximately 6,000,000,000,000 miles.)

A glossary of Star Wars terms:

ICBM - Intercontinental Ballistic Missiles
ASAT - Anti-satellite weapons
SAINT - Satellite Interceptor Program
ABM - Anti-Ballistic Missile
SIS - Satellite Interceptor System
MHV - Miniature Homing Vehicle
DSCS - Defense Satellite Communications System
DEW - Distance Early Warning
FLTSATCOM - Fleet Satellite Communications System
MILSTAR - Military Strategic Tactical and Relay System
ELINT - U.S. Electronic Intelligence
RORSAT - Radar Ocean Reconnaissance Satellite System
NOSS - Navy Ocean Surveillance Satellite System
GPS - Global Positioning System
IMEWS - Integrated Missile Early Warning System
SRAM - Short Range Attack Missile
SDI - Strategic Defense Initiative